WORLD ALMANAC® LIBRARY OF THE STATES

Indiana

THE HOOSIER STATE

by Lynn Brunelle

Curriculum Consultant: Jean Craven,
Director of Instructional Support,
Albuquerque, NM, Public Schools

WORLD ALMANAC® LIBRARY

Please visit our web site at: www.worldalmanaclibrary.com
For a free color catalog describing World Almanac® Library's list of high-quality books
and multimedia programs, call 1-800-848-2928 or fax your request to (414) 332-3567.

Library of Congress Cataloging-in-Publication Data

Brunelle, Lynn.
      Indiana, the Hoosier State / by Lynn Brunelle.
          p. cm. — (World Almanac Library of the states)
      Includes bibliographical references and index.
      Summary: Illustrations and text present the history, geography, people, politics and
government, economy, and social life and customs of Indiana, whose motto is "The
Crossroads of America."
      ISBN 0-8368-5116-1 (lib. bdg.)
      ISBN 0-8368-5285-0 (softcover)
      1. Indiana—Juvenile literature. [1. Indiana.] I. Title. II. Series.
F526.3.B78   2002
977.2—dc21   2001046988

This edition first published in 2002 by
World Almanac® Library
330 West Olive Street, Suite 100
Milwaukee, WI 53212 USA

Design and Editorial: **Jack&Bill**/Bill SMITH STUDIO Inc.
Editors: Jackie Ball and Kristen Behrens
Art Directors: Ron Leighton and Jeffrey Rutzky
Photo Research and Buying: Christie Silver and Sean Livingstone
Design and Production: Maureen O'Connor and Jeffrey Rutzky
World Almanac® Library Editors: Patricia Lantier, Amy Stone, Valerie J. Weber,
Catherine Gardner, Carolyn Kott Washburne, Alan Wachtel, Monica Rausch
World Almanac® Library Production: Scott M. Krall, Eva Erato-Rudek, Tammy Gruenewald

Photo credits: p. 4; p. 6 (top) © Corel, (bottom) © Painet; p. 7 (bottom) © ArtToday, (top)
© PhotoDisc; p. 9 © Historical Picture Archive/CORBIS; p. 10 © Lake County Museum/CORBIS;
p. 11 © ArtToday; p. 12 © ArtToday; p. 13 © Library of Congress; p. 14; p. 15 © Corel; p. 17 © Bob
Rowan; p. 18 © Progressive Image/CORBIS; p. 19 © Larry Freid/TimePix; p. 20 CVB, CVB,
© Painet; p. 21 © PhotoDisc, PhotoDisc, © Corel; p. 26 (all) © PhotoDisc; p. 27 © PNI; p. 29
© Joseph Sohm; Visions of America/CORBIS; p. 30 Courtesy of the Indiana Legislature; p. 31 (top
left) © David Allocca/TimePix; p. 31 (all) © Library of Congress; p. 32 © Pictoral Parade/TimePix;
p. 33 © Brent Smith/TimePix; p. 34 © Tom G Lynn/TimePix; p. 35 (top) © Time Magazine/TimePix,
(bottom) © Corel; p. 36 © PhotoDisc; p. 37 © Painet; p. 38 © PhotoDisc; p. 39 (top) © PhotoDisc,
(bottom) © PhotoDisc; p. 40 © PhotoDisc; p. 41 (top) © Jacksons Kevin Winter; DMI/TimePix,
(bottom) © Corel; p. 42 © Library of Congress; p. 44 (left) © Corel, (right) © Artville; p. 45 (left)
© Artville, (right) © Corel

Indiana

INTRODUCTION	4
ALMANAC	6
HISTORY	8
THE PEOPLE	16
THE LAND	20
ECONOMY & COMMERCE	24
POLITICS & GOVERNMENT	28
CULTURE & LIFESTYLE	32
NOTABLE PEOPLE	38
TIME LINE	42
STATE EVENTS & ATTRACTIONS	44
MORE ABOUT INDIANA	46
INDEX	47

At the Crossroads

Located in the U.S. heartland, Indiana calls itself "The Crossroads of America." With more miles of interstate highway per square mile than any other state, and five interstate routes converging within its borders, two-thirds of the U.S. population is within a day's drive.

Those roads are well-traveled. Before the Civil War Indiana was a crucial station on the Underground Railroad, which helped thousands of southern slaves flee north to freedom. As industry boomed roads took steel, gas, and automobiles from Indiana all over the nation.

Indiana roads have even led Indiana people on their way to stardom. Cole Porter traveled to New York in the 1920s and conquered Broadway by defining American popular music. Steve McQueen and James Dean went to Hollywood in the '40s and became movie stars. Of all the roads taken in Indiana, at least one was entirely new. In 1903 Wilbur Wright, another Indianan, and his brother Orville (born in Ohio), forged an entirely new road — high in the sky. The Wright brothers built and flew the world's first airplane and are remembered as aviation pioneers.

Of course a crossroads is not just a point of departure, but of arrival. For novelist Theodore Dreiser, Indiana provided the formative experiences behind his great American novel, *An American Tragedy.* Kurt Vonnegut, author of *Slaughterhouse Five,* has described his experience as a "Native Middle Westerner" as both culturally rich and plainly American. Talk show host David Letterman agrees, "There's something about Indiana — a lack of suspicion or anxiety or edginess in the people."

Many people think of Indiana as the most southern in character of the northern states. Much of Indiana's early settlement was by immigrants from the "hills to the south," and according to one theory the Indiana nickname *Hoosier* may have come from these Southerners, who called the hills "hoozers."

▶ Map of Indiana, showing interstate highway system, as well as major cities and waterways.

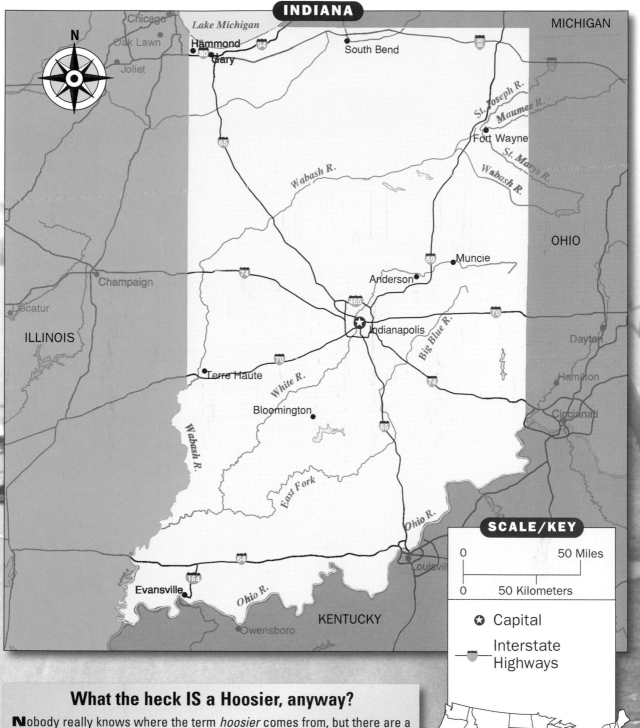

INDIANA

MICHIGAN

Lake Michigan

Chicago
Oak Lawn
Hammond
Gary
Joliet
South Bend

St. Joseph R.
Maumee R.
Fort Wayne
St. Marys R.
Wabash R.

OHIO

Wabash R.

Champaign

Muncie
Anderson

Decatur

ILLINOIS

Indianapolis
Dayton

Terre Haute
White R.

Big Blue R.

Hamilton

Bloomington

Cincinnati

Wabash R.

East Fork

Ohio R.

Louisville

Evansville

Ohio R.

KENTUCKY

Owensboro

SCALE/KEY

0 ———— 50 Miles

0 ———— 50 Kilometers

⭐ Capital

Interstate Highways

What the heck IS a Hoosier, anyway?

Nobody really knows where the term *hoosier* comes from, but there are a lot of theories. Some think it's slang for "who's yer?," or "Who's here?" Others think it is a variation on "husher," for someone who can hush a brawl. Still others believe it's named after a contractor named Samuel Hoosier, who hired his workers from Indiana. There are also those who hold it comes from pioneer days when Southerners called hills "hoozers."

Fast Facts

Indiana (IN), The Hoosier State

Entered Union

December 11, 1816 (19th state)

Capital	Population
Indianapolis	791,926

Total Population

6,080,485 (14th most populous state)

Largest Cities	Population
Indianapolis	791,926
Fort Wayne	205,727
Evansville	121,582
South Bend	107,789
Gary	102,746

Land Area

35,867 square miles (92,896 square kilometers) (38th largest state)

State Motto

"The Crossroads of America" — *Indiana earned its state motto during the early 1800s. At that time it was mostly river traffic along the Ohio River that crossed through the state. Later, twelve different stagecoach lines passed through Indiana.*

State Song

"On the Banks of the Wabash, Far Away," by Paul Dresser

State Tree

Tulip tree, also known as the yellow poplar (lirodendrum tulipifera) — *This popular tree is also the state tree of Kentucky and Tennessee, and its greenish-yellow blossoms were once also Indiana's state flower.*

State Flower

Peony — *Indiana had three former state flowers before finally settling on the peony in 1957.*

State Stone

Limestone — *The city of Bedford is known as the limestone capital of the world. Its quarries have helped construct many of the nation's most famous buildings, including the Empire State Building in New York and the Tribune Tower in Chicago.*

State Bird

Cardinal — *Also known as the Red Bird, its glorious song is commonly heard in forests, fields, and even city gardens.*

State Poem

"Indiana" by Arthur Franklin

State Insect

Say's Firefly has been proposed as Indiana's official state insect. This firefly was named by Thomas Say, Indiana's famous naturalist, in 1824.

PLACES TO VISIT

Lincoln Boyhood National Memorial, *Lincoln City*
Abraham Lincoln lived here with his family from 1816 to 1830. The National Memorial is centered on the cabin site, near the grave of his mother, Nancy Hanks Lincoln. The Lincoln Living Historical Farm is a working pioneer homestead with a cabin, outbuildings, animals, and gardens.

Holiday World Theme Park, *Santa Claus*
Claiming to be the nation's first theme park, Holiday World was once known as Santa Claus Land but has branched out from Christmas to include Halloween and Fourth of July themes.

Wyandotte Cave, near *Wyandotte*
With 25 miles (40 kilometers) of passages on five levels, this is the largest of many caves in the region. The cave was used by Native Americans and is believed to have been inhabited in prehistoric times.

For other places and events, see p. 44 For other places and events, see p. 44

BIGGEST, BEST, AND MOST

- Indiana's Lost River runs 22 miles (35 km) underground.
  - Indiana is a leader in the production of musical instruments. In fact, Elkhart is known as "The Musical Instrument Capital of the World."
- Twenty-four percent of the nation's steel is produced in Indiana, more than in any other state. Indiana also leads the world in the manufacture of compact discs and elevators.

STATE FIRSTS

- The American Railway Union, the first industrial union in the United States, was founded in Terre Haute, Indiana, by Eugene V. Debs.
- The first successful goldfish farm in the U.S. opened in Martinsville, Indiana.

Lightning Brought Down from the Heavens

People stood overwhelmed with awe, as if in the presence of the supernatural. The strange, weird light, exceeded in power only by the sun, rendered the square as light as midday. Men fell on their knees, groans were uttered at the sight and many were dumb with amazement. We contemplated the new wonder in science as lightning brought down from the heavens.

Eyewitness account from 1880, when the city of Wabash became the first in the nation to be illuminated by electricity.

Sideburns and Burnsides

Indiana General Ambrose Burnside fought at some of the most famous battles in the Civil War, was elected three times as governor of Rhode Island, and served six years as a U.S. senator. With all that to his name, he is now best remembered for his long, bushy side whiskers, which were once called "burnsides" in his honor. The term later switched around to "sideburns." Nobody knows when or how, but it does seem to make more sense that way.

On the Banks of the Wabash

> Can't get Indiana off my mind,
> That's the place I love to see.
> — *lyrics by Robert De Leon, "Can't Get Indiana Off My Mind"*

Historians estimate that the first humans to arrive in what would become Indiana migrated across North America and settled in the Indiana region as long as twelve thousand years ago. Over time, various tribes formed. The remnants of their cultures can be found in archaeological sites scattered throughout the state.

One of the best preserved is that of Angel Mounds near Evansville. It tells the story of what is known as the Middle Mississippian Culture — a prehistoric culture that existed from about A.D. 1000 to when Europeans first arrived in the mid-1500s.

This culture hunted in the lush river valleys and grew corn, beans, and squash in the fertile lands of the Ohio River. They built their main settlement and its surrounding villages around a huge mound of earth on top of which they placed a temple-like home for their leader. For more than three hundred years, Angel Mounds was the largest settlement in Indiana.

Significant archaeological work has been done at Angel Mounds, and researchers have recovered many artifacts. From these finds, we can draw important conclusions about the way the earliest Indianans lived.

Native American groups such as the Algonquian, the Potawatomi, and the Delaware began to settle in the area. The Algonquian organized all the local tribes into an alliance called the Miami Confederation. Eventually, their strength in unity would be tested during several battles against the Iroquois to help protect their land. The Iroquois were pushed out of their traditional land, to the east of Indiana, by European settlers.

Native Americans of Indiana

- Algonquian
- Atchakangoen
- Delaware
- Iroquois
- Kilatika
- Mengkonia
- Miami
- Ojibwa (Chippewa)
- Ottawa
- Pepikokia
- Piankashaw
- Potawatomi
- Shawnee
- Wea

Valuable Land

Native people were not the only people who saw the rich
land of Indiana as an ideal place to settle. Europeans were
drawn to it as well. In the mid-1500s Spanish explorers led
by Hernando de Soto were the first recorded Europeans to
set foot on Indiana soil. It is believed that de Soto and his
men visited the settlement at Angel Mounds and placed a
cross at the sacred site. In 1671, the French claimed the
land and sent Robert Cavelier, sieur de La Salle, down the
St. Joseph River. For centuries, La Salle's visit was thought
to be the first European advance into Indiana.

▲ A Fort Wayne
postcard, circa 1939.

The French were not the only Europeans with plans to possess Indiana. This area, with its fertile farmland and abundant water supply, was also desired by the British. The French wanted to secure their trade routes from Canada down to Louisiana. The British, along with the American colonists, had set up camp to the east in Pennsylvania and the southeast in what is now the Carolinas. They were pushing to expand their settlements westward to the banks of the Ohio and Wabash Rivers. Through all of this the Native Americans had no intentions of handing over their homeland without a fierce struggle.

Tension Builds

Forts were built, alliances were made, and tensions grew. La Salle and Louis de Baude de Frontenac, the governor of New France (Canada), made a plan to gain control of the Maumee–Wabash fur trade route between Canada and Louisiana. They decided to relocate the Native Americans in the region to a place called Kekionga. Because the Native Americans were collectively known as the Miami Indians, the settlement was renamed Miami Town. Still occupied today, it is now called Fort Wayne and is the oldest continuously occupied community in Indiana.

The power struggle between French, English, and Native Americans escalated. The French built several forts to try and stave off English attacks and to protect their access to the Mississippi River — Fort Philippe (later known as Fort Miami), Fort Ouiatanon, and Fort Vincennes. The English enlisted the help of the Native Americans against the French.

An eyewitness to the fighting in 1687, the Marquis de Seignelay of France, noted in his memoir:

> *The English have begun by the most powerful and best disciplined Indians of all America, whom they have excited entirely against us . . . They also employ the Iroquois to excite all our other Indians against us. They sent those last year to attack the Hurons and the Outawas, our most ancient subjects; from whom they swept by surprise more than seventy-five prisoners, including some of their principal Chiefs; killed several others, and finally offered peace and the restitution of their prisoners, if they would quit the French and acknowledge the English. They sent those Iroquois to attack the Illinois and the Miamis, our allies, who are in the neighborhood of Fort Saint Louis, built by M. de La Salle on the Illinois River which empties into the River Colbert or Mississippi; those Iroquois massacred and burnt a great number of them, and carried off many prisoners with threats of entire extermination if they would not unite with them against the French.*

The French and Indian Wars (1754–1763) were, ironically, between the French and the English. The Native Americans, though they were never again to enjoy the freedom to live peacefully on the land, joined in the battle and eventually helped tip the balance of power.

The Battle of Tippecanoe
November 7, 1811

Major General William Henry Harrison fought an Indian confederacy led by the Shawnee Laulewasikau (Tenskwatawa), also known as the Prophet. The battle took place at Prophetstown, the Indian capital on the Tippecanoe River and the site of the present town of Battle Ground, Indiana. Harrison wanted to destroy the burgeoning Native American alliance being promoted by Laulewasikau and his brother Tecumseh. Harrison's army repelled an Indian counterattack and burned the village. Laulewasikau fled to Canada. Although the two sides suffered equal losses, the battle was widely regarded as a U.S. victory and helped establish Harrison's national reputation.

The Northwest Territory

Finally, in 1763, the British won the French and Indian War and the French surrendered their claims to a large tract of land that became known as the Northwest Territory. This territory included the present states of Ohio, Indiana, Illinois, Michigan, Wisconsin, and part of Minnesota. It officially became a part of the United States when the Treaty of Paris was signed in 1783, ending the Revolutionary War. The first authorized American settlement in the new territory was Clarksville, in southern Indiana.

In 1787, the Continental Congress enacted the Northwest Ordinance, which provided for the Northwest Territory to be presided over by a governor and three judges. The Northwest Ordinance also prohibited future slavery but did not abolish the practice altogether; those already using slave labor were allowed to continue doing so.

Although the war was over, many of the tensions still remained. Native Americans led by Chief Pontiac fought to win back their land. White settlers streamed in from New England, the southern states, and the surrounding lands, squeezing Native populations out. General William Henry Harrison, who later became the ninth president of the United States, was the first governor of the Indiana Territory. Harrison was assigned the task of ending Native American rights to the land through treaties. Agreements were signed at Fort Wayne (1803), Fort Industry (1805), and Grouseland (1805). The Indians of the Miami Confederation

▲ The Treaty of Greenville (1795) was the first with Native Americans to open up any of the region that would become the state of Indiana to white settlement. The treaty granted settlers the right to live in approximately two-thirds of the Ohio region as well as a small sliver of southeastern Indiana.

DID YOU KNOW?

President Abraham Lincoln spent most of his boyhood in Spencer County, Indiana. He was eight when he moved there and twenty-one when he moved to Illinois. His boyhood home is now a museum open to the public.

continued to fight for their rights to their land. They were defeated by Harrison and his troops at the Battle of Tippecanoe in 1811, bringing an end to most Indian resistance in the territory. By 1840 the major Native American tribes abandoned the area. Today "the land of the Indians" has fewer than sixteen thousand Native American inhabitants.

Indiana Statehood, Expansion, and the Civil War

The end of Native American rebellion marked a huge increase in settlement. In 1816, Indiana officially became a state. Jonathan Jennings was elected the first Indiana governor, and Corydon served as the state capital until 1825, when Indianapolis was granted the title.

From 1816 to 1850 Indiana was settled by families from Virginia, Kentucky, New England, and the Carolinas, by immigrants from Sweden, Germany, and Ireland, and also by Quakers from the South who left in protest over the slavery debate.

Crossroads to Freedom

In the 1850s opinions about slavery divided the United States, and the Civil War loomed on the horizon. Indiana was divided. The northern part of the state, with its many Quakers and newcomers from New England, was supportive of the Union and intensely opposed slavery. The southern part of the state had more farmers and pioneers who defended the right to own slaves. The state constitution, written mostly by Southerners, made assisting slaves seeking freedom illegal. Those who helped slaves were considered criminals under the law.

This didn't matter to Levi and Katie Coffin. The Coffins were citizens of the quiet farming community of Fountain City and were part of an organized underground movement that helped slaves escape to freedom. Members of this movement, known as the Underground Railroad, hid escaping slaves in their houses, barns, cellars, and shops. Levi Coffin, known as "President of the Underground Railroad," and Katie defied Indiana state law and helped more than two thousand runaway slaves escape to freedom in the North. Because of the Coffins' efforts, Fountain City

The Underground Railroad

Many people offered assistance to fugitive slaves along what was known as the Underground Railroad. African Americans had an important hand in the operations that ran through Indiana. Some, such as Elijah Anderson, even went to the southern states to rescue slaves. He was caught during one of those expeditions and died in prison in Kentucky. African-American communities in Jefferson County, along the Ohio River, were particularly important because they helped fugitive slaves cross the river. Station houses would then provide shelter, food, and clothing to the runaway slaves as they proceeded farther north. The most famous of these was "Grand Central Station," in Fountain City, Indiana, run by the Quakers Levi and Katie Coffin (pictured above). Some former slaves also settled in Indiana.

was known as the "Grand Central Station" of the Underground Railroad.

When the Civil War broke out in 1861, many Indiana citizens pledged their allegiance to President Lincoln (a one-time Indianan). Almost two hundred thousand soldiers went into battle — only New York sent more men — and helped win the fight to abolish slavery and keep the nation from splitting in two.

Getting Connected

In 1865 the Civil War ended. Indiana entered into a period of fast growth. Agriculture and industry began to flourish in the 1860s. Efficient transportation opened up a world of possibilities. Railroads, rivers, roads, and canals crisscrossed the country and linked the North, South, East, and West. Indiana was at the center of it all, earning its nickname, "The Crossroads of America." Indiana corn, grains, soybeans, cattle, and hogs were exported throughout the country. Limestone was quarried and sent off to cities to be crafted into buildings. The Empire State Building, Rockefeller Center, the Pentagon, the U.S. Treasury, and fourteen state capitols are built from Indiana limestone.

Love Thy Neighbor

Trusting that this volume will accomplish something toward the eradication of caste, which still exists in our land — though, in the providence of God, slavery itself has been removed — and in the acceptance and practice of that command, which reads, "Love thy neighbor as thyself," I now commend it to the reader.

Levi Coffin, preface to Reminiscences of Levi Coffin, the reputed president of the Underground Railroad

▼ The Levi Coffin House.

Levi Coffin House

A new crop of Indiana enterprise spurred the state's economy. Businesses such as The Ball Jar Company and Van de Kamp's Pork and Beans, and innovations such as the first gasoline pump by Sylvanus Bowser and the hardened steel plow by James Oliver, played a key role. Also, when natural gas was discovered in the state, there was no chance of slowing Indiana down.

Today Indiana lives up to its motto, "The Crossroads of America." It has more miles of interstate highway and more major highway intersections, than any other state in the nation.

Indiana at the Turn of the Century

Two major industries have carried Indiana into the new millennium — steelmaking and automobile manufacturing — but neither without a little rust. More than two hundred different makes of cars were produced in Indiana between 1900 and 1920, from Duesenbergs, Studebakers, Auburns, and Stutzes, to Maxwells — all considered precious antiques today.

In general, both the steel and the automobile industries took a beating after the recession in the 1980s. Some enterprises, such as General Electric, Central Soya, and even General Motors, fared better than others and helped offset the economic damage caused by the recession.

Today industry is alive and well in Indiana. The state has a strong economy anchored in a diverse range of manufacturing enterprises and service industries. The state has also invested more in educational facilities, and many cities have begun redevelopment projects, spurring a building boom in some areas.

▼ A 1923 Studebaker.

Most Southern of Northern States

> I have such fondness for Indiana. There's something about Indiana—a lack of suspicion or anxiety or edginess in the people—that you don't get here.
>
> — *David Letterman*

Though the name *Indiana* means "land of the Indians," there are fewer than sixteen thousand Native Americans who still make their home there. Of the more than six million residents of Indiana (ranking it the fourteenth most populous state in the nation), the vast majority were born in the United States.

A New Land

There were three major waves of settlement. The first came from the southern states as frontiersmen and pioneers settled the land after the French and Indian War. Fiercely independent, these early settlers brought with them an ethic for hard work and a love for small-town life.

The next wave of immigration was concentrated in the northern part of the state and consisted of settlers from New York, New England, and Pennsylvania. With this

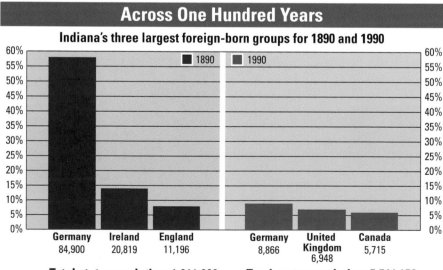

Across One Hundred Years

Indiana's three largest foreign-born groups for 1890 and 1990

■ 1890   ■ 1990

| Germany 84,900 | Ireland 20,819 | England 11,196 | Germany 8,866 | United Kingdom 6,948 | Canada 5,715 |

Total state population: 1,911,896
Total foreign-born: 146,205 (8%)

Total state population: 5,544,159
Total foreign-born: 94,263 (2%)

Patterns of Immigration

The total number of people who immigrated to Indiana in 1998 was 3,981. Of that number, the largest immigrant groups were from Mexico (22%), India (9%), and China (5%).

group came a small population of Amish and Mennonites that still maintain communities in the northeastern part of the state.

The third wave was the smallest. It was made up of European immigrants and African Americans who flocked to Indiana at the turn of the century seeking work in the steel mills and other industrial factories.

The successive waves of immigration from primarily European countries to Indiana mean that the population as a whole is not diverse. Industrial cities to the north have the highest concentration of ethnic diversity, contrasting strongly with the urban areas that lie along the Ohio River and the more rural areas in between.

Age Distribution in Indiana	
0–4	423,215
5–19	1,340,171
20–24	425,731
25–44	1,791,828
45–64	2,202,993
65 and over	752,831

Heritage and Background, Indiana — Year 2000

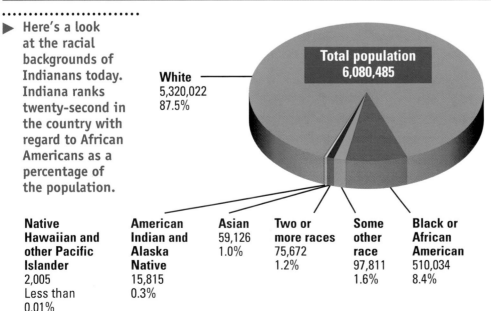

▶ Here's a look at the racial backgrounds of Indianans today. Indiana ranks twenty-second in the country with regard to African Americans as a percentage of the population.

Total population 6,080,485

White 5,320,022 87.5%

Note: 3.5% (214,536) of the population identify themselves as **Hispanic** or **Latino,** a cultural designation that crosses racial lines. Hispanics and Latinos are counted in this category and the racial category of their choice.

Native Hawaiian and other Pacific Islander 2,005 Less than 0.01%

American Indian and Alaska Native 15,815 0.3%

Asian 59,126 1.0%

Two or more races 75,672 1.2%

Some other race 97,811 1.6%

Black or African American 510,034 8.4%

Educational Levels of Indianans Age 25 and Over	
Less than 9th grade	297,423
9th to 12th grade, no diploma	552,591
High school graduate, including equivalency	1,333,093
Some college, no degree	578,205
Associate degree	184,717
Bachelor's degree	321,278
Graduate or professional degree	221,663

Kurt Vonnegut describes the particularly American character of Indiana in his essay "To Be a Native Middle Westerner":

New York and Boston and other ports on the Atlantic have Europe for an influential, often importunate neighbor. Middle Westerners do not. Many of us of European ancestry are on that account ignorant of our families' past in the Old World and the culture there. Our only heritage is American. When Germans captured me during the Second World War, one asked me, "Why are you making war against your brothers?" I didn't have a clue what he was talking about. Anglo-Americans and African Americans, whose ancestors came to the Middle West from the South, commonly have a much more compelling awareness of a homeland elsewhere in the past than do I — in Dixie, of course, not the British Isles or Africa.

Citizens of Indiana are thus generally at least two steps removed from their immigrant ancestry. By one path or another, they have all found themselves at "The Crossroads of America."

▼ Downtown Indianapolis, Indiana's most populous city.

Religion

Of Indianans who are adherents of particular religions, more than half belong to Protestant Christian churches. Methodists make up 18 percent of the state's population. Other Protestant denominations represented in Indiana include Baptist, Episcopalian, Church of the Nazarene, Lutheran, Mennonite, and Unitarian, to name but a few. About 2.9 percent of the Indiana population are Quaker, and many of those Indianans who opposed slavery in the nineteenth century were as well. Among those Indianans who are not Protestant, 12.6 percent are Catholic and more than twenty thousand are Jewish.

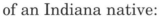

▲ Famous Hoosier James Dean.

Where Do Hoosiers Live?

Most people in Indiana live in cities, suburbs, and towns. Indianapolis is the largest city, but there are several other metropolitan areas scattered throughout the state. About a third of the population lives in rural farm areas.

A number of famous people called Indiana home, from legends like Johnny Appleseed, Knute Rockne, and Jimmy Hoffa to musicians as diverse as Cole Porter and The Jackson Five. Indiana has also fostered great writers such as Kurt Vonnegut and Theodore Dreiser as well as comedians Red Skelton and David Letterman. Screen icons James Dean and Steve McQueen and one of the innovators of modern dance, Twyla Tharp, hail from the Hoosier State.

Writer Theodore Dreiser summed up the character of an Indiana native:

I insist that the Hoosier is different mentally and spiritually from the average American. He is softer, less sophisticated, more poetic . . . He dreams a lot. He likes to play in simple ways . . . He has the temperament of the artist.

A Rich and Rugged Landscape

> . . . it has been esteemed by intelligent men, who have often traversed it, in all directions, in point of rural scenery, a copious supply of pure water, fertility of soil and security to health, equal to any part of the western country . . .
>
> — *Edmund Dana, employed as a guide for immigrants, 1819*

From the sand dunes and white beaches along the shores of Lake Michigan to the valleys and cliffs of the Cumberland Mountains to the millions of acres of rolling farmland in between, there's a bit of everything in Indiana. The highest elevation in Indiana is along the Ohio border, at 1,257 feet (383 km) above sea level; the lowest, at 320 feet (98 meters), is in the southwest where the Wabash River enters the Ohio River. The majority — as much as 90 percent of the land — lies between 500 and 1,000 feet (152 and 305 m) above sea level.

Climate

In general, Indiana has very cold winters and hot, humid summers. The land nearest to Lake Michigan, however, benefits by that proximity. The lake's waters are warm and generally ensure that summers are a little cooler and winters a little warmer than the rest of the state. That proximity also means that the northern part of Indiana receives much more snowfall in the winter months. The area averages 40 inches (102 centimeters) each year.

▼ *From left to right*: **A misty vista at Brown County State Park; grapevines at the Chateau Pomije Winery; barge traffic on the Ohio River; Sam Smith's covered bridge; sunset on Lake Michigan; on the banks of the Blue River.**

Home, Home on the Plains

The soil is well adapted to maize, wheat, oats, rye, hemp, and tobacco. The country is admirably fitted for rearing cattle and swine, having great abundance of acorns and roots on which they feed.
— David Baillie Warden, 1819

This observation, made nearly two hundred years ago, still remains true today. The majority of the state consists of two fertile plains, both of which are highly productive agricultural regions.

In the north, along the Great Lakes, are the Great Lakes Plains, also known as the Northern Lake and Moraine Region. As little as twelve thousand years ago, the most recent ice age ended and glaciers retreated from the land. As they departed from this region of Indiana, they left behind dark, rich soil, perfect for farming. Many small lakes were created, too, originally filled by water from the melting glaciers. The Great Lakes Plains are separated by North America's east–west divide. To the west, the rivers flow into the Mississippi River. To the east, they run to the St. Lawrence.

Indiana's central plains are called the Till Plains of the Midwestern Corn Belt. Glaciers also covered this region during the most recent ice age. Extremely fertile, this agricultural belt contains many large farms that produce corn, soybeans, and wheat, as well as support grazing livestock such as cattle. While the region is not mountainous, there are low hills and shallow valleys. The highest point in Indiana is in the eastern Till Plains.

As a whole, the state consists of 23 million acres (9,308,100 hectares), of which 15.1 million acres (6,110,970 ha) are farmland — 68 percent of the total land area.

Average January temperature
Indianapolis: 27° F (-2.7° C)
Fort Wayne: 24° F (-4° C)

Average July temperature
Indianapolis: 76° F (24° C)
Fort Wayne: 74° F (23° C)

Average yearly rainfall
Indianapolis: 40.2 inches (102 cm)
Fort Wayne: 36.2 inches (91 cm)

Average yearly snowfall
Indianapolis: 22.7 inches (57 cm)
Fort Wayne: 32.9 inches (83 cm)

Highest Elevation
1,257 feet (383 m) (Wayne County)

Lowest Elevation
320 feet (98 m) (Posey County)

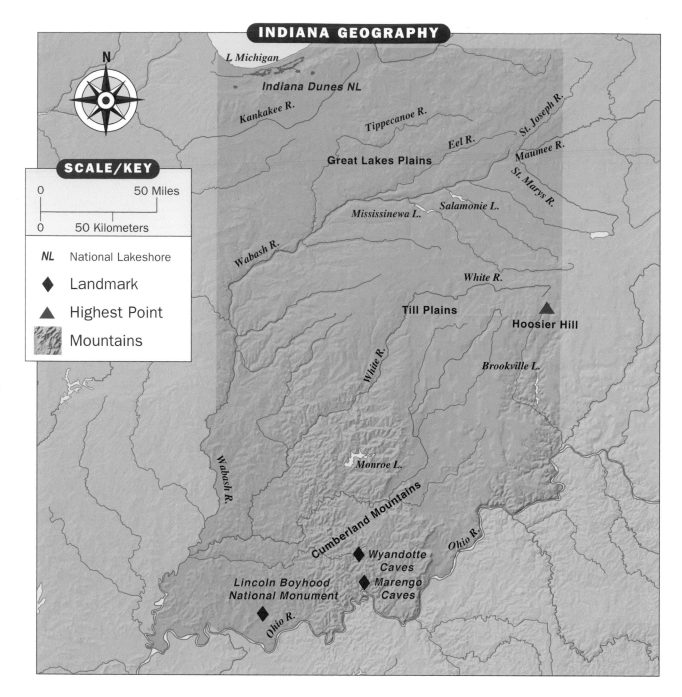

INDIANA GEOGRAPHY

L Michigan

Indiana Dunes NL

Kankakee R.

Tippecanoe R.

Eel R.

St. Joseph R.

Maumee R.

St. Marys R.

Great Lakes Plains

Mississinewa L.

Salamonie L.

Wabash R.

White R.

Till Plains

▲ Hoosier Hill

Brookville L.

White R.

Monroe L.

Cumberland Mountains

Ohio R.

◆ Wyandotte Caves

◆ Marengo Caves

Lincoln Boyhood National Monument

◆

Ohio R.

Wabash R.

SCALE/KEY

0   50 Miles

0   50 Kilometers

NL   National Lakeshore

◆   Landmark

▲   Highest Point

   Mountains

Hills and Lowlands

The glaciers of the most recent ice age that scoured and flattened the majority of the rest of the state did not make it to south-central Indiana. As a result, this region has several series of steep hills interspersed with stretches of lowland.

To the southwest there are coal and petroleum deposits. The region also contains underground streams, some of which have washed through limestone deposits and created

Major Rivers

Wabash River
529 miles (851 km)

White River
255 miles (410 km)

Tippecanoe River
166 miles (267 km)

caves. The Marengo Caves, in Marengo, and the Wyandotte Caves, in Leavenworth, are major tourist attractions and contain spectacular limestone formations.

Lakes and Rivers

Lake Michigan forms 45 miles (72 km) of Indiana's northern border, while the state's southern border is defined by the Ohio River. That is not, however, the only Indiana border to be defined by water.

Indiana's major river is the Wabash, which flows southwest across the state. Beginning at the city of Terre Haute, it forms 200 miles (320 km) of Indiana's border with Illinois before flowing into the Ohio River. In earlier centuries the river was used by the French to travel between Louisiana and Quebec. Later flatboats and steamships traveled the river, transporting goods. By the late 1850s, however, the river was no longer a commercial route. The railroads, and then automotive vehicles, were used instead.

Two of Indiana's other major rivers are the White and the Tippecanoe. The Tippecanoe is famous for being the site where Major General William Henry Harrison defeated the Shawnee on November 7, 1811. Both are major branches of the Wabash. Several other important Wabash tributaries include the Eel, Mississinewa, and Salamonie Rivers.

The St. Joseph and the St. Marys Rivers join at Fort Wayne to form the Maumee, which flows past the city and empties into Lake Erie.

Save the Dunes

The authorization of Indiana Dunes National Lakeshore was the culmination of a fifty-year fight to save the dunes that lie along the shores of Lake Michigan. They were being destroyed by industrialization. Establishing the dunes as a protected area led to the acquisition of 8,329 acres (3,371 ha) of dunes and wetlands. The lakeshore is on a bird migratory route and surrounds the state park on three sides. It features long beaches; high dunes, some as high as 200 feet (61 m); wooded ravines, lagoons, and swamps; and bogs that are remnants of ice age glaciers. The dunes are also home to a wide range of unusual plants — from arctic mosses to desert cactuses.

▼ **The Indiana Dunes along Lake Michigan.**

Wheels and Steel

> It is when you have done your work honestly, when you have contributed your share to the common fund that you begin to live.
>
> — *Eugene V. Debs, 1908*

One of the most important factors in Indiana's economic success is location, location, location. That's right. Geography. Indiana is within 800 miles (1,287 kilometers) of forty of the top fifty U.S. consumer and industrial markets. With one of the nation's best interstate highway systems, a large labor force, and abundant natural resources, Indiana's manufacturing and shipping is the backbone of its economic success.

The proximity to so many markets, and a solid transportation system that includes not only roads but also shipping lanes, railroads, and airports, means that Indiana-made goods can easily make their way through the rest of the state to the rest of the nation and the world.

Manufacturing

For over one hundred years, Indiana has been manufacturing steel. In fact, Indiana is responsible for 24 percent of all U.S. steel production. One-quarter of all the jobs in Indiana are manufacturing-based and bring in over 40 percent of all household income.

While it helps to be situated at "The Crossroads of America," Indiana has an abundant variety of manufactured goods. Elkhart is well known for producing musical instruments as well as being considered the world center for RV (recreational vehicle) manufacturing. The city is home to the RV Hall of Fame.

Fort Wayne produces much of the world's supply of diamond tools. Office furniture, batteries, elevators, CDs, and prescription drugs are just a few more of the other items produced in this state.

Top Employers (of workers age sixteen and over)
Manufacturing... 24.3%
Service............... 19.7%
Wholesale and retail trade.......... 17.9%
Government........ 12.6%
Finance, insurance and real estate.... 5.5%
Transportation, communication, public utilities...... 5.1%
Construction........ 4.5%
Agriculture........... 2.2%

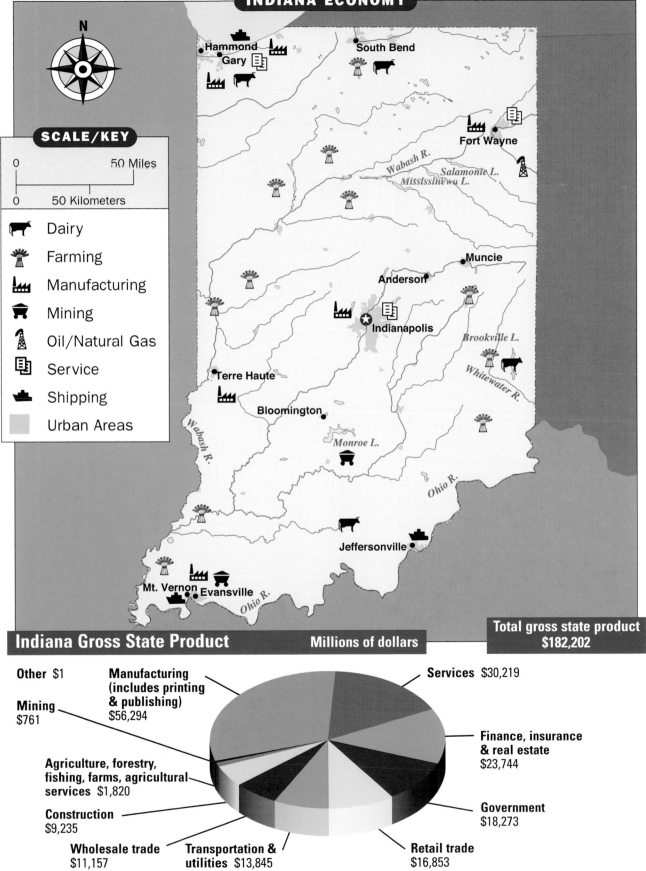

INDIANA ECONOMY

SCALE/KEY

0 — 50 Miles
0 — 50 Kilometers

- 🐄 Dairy
- 🌾 Farming
- 🏭 Manufacturing
- 🛒 Mining
- 🛢 Oil/Natural Gas
- 📑 Service
- 🚢 Shipping
- ⬜ Urban Areas

Hammond
Gary
South Bend
Fort Wayne
Salamonie L.
Mississinewa L.
Wabash R.
Muncie
Anderson
Indianapolis
Brookville L.
Whitewater R.
Terre Haute
Bloomington
Monroe L.
Ohio R.
Wabash R.
Jeffersonville
Mt. Vernon
Evansville
Ohio R.

Indiana Gross State Product — Millions of dollars

Total gross state product $182,202

- Other $1
- Manufacturing (includes printing & publishing) $56,294
- Mining $761
- Agriculture, forestry, fishing, farms, agricultural services $1,820
- Construction $9,235
- Wholesale trade $11,157
- Transportation & utilities $13,845
- Retail trade $16,853
- Government $18,273
- Finance, insurance & real estate $23,744
- Services $30,219

▲ *From left to right:* **Steel being manufactured; compact discs.**

Because of its huge labor force, Indiana has a deep involvement in the labor movement. Eugene V. Debs founded the United States's first industrial union, The American Railway Union, in Terre Haute in 1893. The Teamsters Union, which has grown to be the largest union in the U.S., was led by Jimmy Hoffa, the son of an Indiana coal worker.

Natural Resources

If you've ever been to New York City and visited the Empire State Building, or taken a trip to the Pentagon in Washington, D.C., you've seen a little piece of Indiana. The limestone that was used in these buildings — as well as fourteen state capitol buildings — was mined and shipped from Indiana. Large deposits of coal in the southwest part of the state provide Indiana's leading source of energy, though a close second is nuclear energy. Of all the states in the nation, Indiana draws the highest percentage of its power from nuclear sources.

The Gas Belt

In the 1880s a huge pocket of natural gas was discovered underground in the central part of the state. The gas lured factories that relied on heat for making products — such as glass. By the late 1880s over one hundred glass-making factories had sprung up. The gas, however, was short-lived and eventually disappeared. So did many of the factories — all except the Ball Jar Company. It switched to using coal and continued producing its glass jars until the 1990s. Now Ball is known for plastic and metal containers and aerospace technology. It has contributed major funding to Ball State University in Muncie.

Agriculture

Indiana ranks among the top ten farming states in the United States, producing such crops as corn, soybeans, wheat, hay, tobacco, and oats. In fact, without Indiana, your movie theater experience wouldn't be as fun because Indiana leads the nation in production of popcorn. Popcorn king Orville Redenbacher is a native of Valparaiso, where an annual popcorn festival is held every year in September.

Vegetables such as cucumbers, cabbage, and potatoes, as well as fruits like apples and melons are also produced in Indiana. Cattle and hogs make up an important piece of Indiana's agriculture. In fact, canned pork and beans was invented by an Indiana grocer's wife named Mrs. Van Camp.

▲ Indiana produces more popcorn than any other state or nation.

Transportation

With more miles of interstate highway per square mile than any other state, it's no surprise that transportation itself is a major industry in Indiana. Many national moving companies are based there because of the easy access to so many highways. These highways also provide jobs for construction workers who build and maintain the roads. But highways aren't the only way people, vegetables, livestock, limestone, steel, and other goods are moved around. Railroads have been hauling goods and people in, out, and around Indiana since 1838, when the first steam railroad rolled through. Water is another avenue for transport. The northern border of Indiana lies along Lake Michigan and provides access to the St. Lawrence Seaway and beyond that, the Atlantic Ocean. Goods also flow in and out of the Port of Indiana, which lies just south of the Indiana Dunes National Lakeshore. Along Indiana's southern border, the Ohio River carries goods to the Mississippi River, where they can travel as far as the Gulf of Mexico.

Major Airports		
Airport	**Location**	**Passengers per year** (approx.)
Indianapolis International Airport	Indianapolis	7,774,908
South Bend Regional Airport	South Bend	865,876
Fort Wayne International Airport	Fort Wayne	714,628

DID YOU KNOW?

The Ohio River, which links Indiana with the Mississippi River system, carries more low-cost freight than the Panama Canal.

Mother of Vice Presidents

> No law shall authorize any debt to be contracted, on behalf of the State, except in the following cases: to meet casual deficits in the revenue; to pay the interest on the State Debt; to repel invasion, suppress insurrection, or, if hostilities be threatened, provide for the public defense.
>
> — *Indiana State Constitution Article 10*

I ndiana makes its money through service industries, manufacturing, transportation, and farming. This makes for a variety of interests in the voting public. Agricultural and environmental concerns can often conflict with those of industry. The state has a significant amount of natural resources that are mined and parkland that is preserved. This is another source for conflicting interests in the political arena.

On the whole, Indiana is a conservative state that, for most of the 1900s, had Republican representation. More recently, however, Democrats have seen some representation: Senator Evan Bayh and Governor Frank O'Bannon were both Democrats.

When you get to the voting public, studies show that the state is evenly balanced with one-third Republican, one-third Democrat, and one-third on the fence. These fence-sitters are swing voters who can go either way in any given election. The Republicans generally are found in the northern areas of the state, where industrial and manufacturing interests are strong. The southern agricultural and urban areas seem to be more Democratic.

A Constitution with Longevity

On the whole, Indiana, whose capital has been at Indianapolis since 1825, still abides by the state constitution that was adopted in 1851. It is no surprise that this constitution states that governors be elected to a four-year term, but Indiana governors can only serve two terms

Indiana State Constitution

*T*o the end, that justice be established, public order maintained, and liberty perpetuated; WE, the People of the State of Indiana, grateful to ALMIGHTY GOD for the free exercise of the right to choose our own form of government, do ordain this Constitution.

February 10, 1851

DID YOU KNOW?

*A*s a result of the 2000 U.S. Census, Indiana lost one seat in the U.S. House of Representatives, giving it nine House seats and eleven electoral votes in presidential elections.

Top Elected Posts in the Executive Branch		
Office	Length of Term	Term Limits
Governor	4 years	2 terms in a 12-year period
Lieutenant Governor	4 years	2 terms in a 12-year period
Attorney General	4 years	2 terms in a 12-year period

in a row. Only Louisiana (1812) and New Jersey (1844) have had gubernatorial term limits for a longer period of time than Indiana.

Indiana's executive, legislative, and judicial branches are similar to those of other states, but there are a few subtle differences.

Executive Branch

Checks and balances are the keystone to any government, and Indiana's structure is no different. First of all, governors can only serve two terms (eight years) in a twelve-year period. The governor can veto, or reject, any new legislation that comes along, but that veto can be canceled if the Senate and House of Representatives vote against it. What is unique under the Indiana constitution is that the governor has the power to appoint or remove any head of any department or governing board and to decide how much each appointee gets paid.

▼ The Indiana Capitol building in downtown Indianapolis.

The governor is not the only elected official in the executive branch. Altogether eight officers are voted into office every four years.

Legislative Branch

The legislature in Indiana is known as the General Assembly, and it is *bicameral* (consisting of two houses, like the U.S. Congress). In Indiana the houses are also called the Senate and the House of Representatives. Unlike the governor, neither senators nor representatives have limits on the number of terms they may serve. The General Assembly meets only once a year, beginning in January and ending in March or April.

In order to change or amend the Indiana constitution, the legislature first has to propose the amendment and both houses then have to approve it. After that the amendment is voted on by the citizens in an election.

Judicial Branch

The judicial branch is like a pyramid. At the top is the highest court — the state Supreme Court, which is made up of a chief justice and four associate justices chosen by the governor. New judges serve for two years, then the public votes to keep them or not. If the public votes to keep them at their post, they can serve up to ten years. Under the Supreme Court are the three branches of the Court of Appeals, which is made up of twelve judges representing three regions in Indiana. Below that are the courts that serve the individual counties — circuit, superior, municipal, and county courts.

Local Government

The government is not just in Washington, D.C., or in the state capital. In Indiana there are four different types of local government. From largest to smallest, they are the county, township, municipality, and school district.

Mother of Vice Presidents

Although Benjamin Harrison was the only Indianan who was elected president, there have been five men from Indiana that served as vice president, earning the state the nickname "Mother of Vice Presidents."

General Assembly			
House	Number of Members	Length of Term	Term Limits
Senate	50 senators	4 years	None
House of Representatives	100 representatives	2 years	None

The White House via Indiana

One Indianan has served as president of the United States

BENJAMIN HARRISON (1889–1893)
Benjamin Harrison holds the honor of being the only president to hail from the state of Indiana. (Although born in Ohio, he spent his adult life in the Hoosier state.) Elected as the twenty-third president of the United States, Harrison, a Republican, was born with politics in his blood. His great-grandfather was one of the signers of the Declaration of Independence. His father was a congressman, and his grandfather, William Henry Harrison, was the country's ninth president, who unfortunately died of pneumonia after being in office for only one month.

Harrison held the first Pan-American Conference in 1889, which forged trade and diplomatic ties between the United States and Latin American countries.

On the domestic front, Harrison helped pass the Dependent Pension Act, establishing funds for disabled Civil War veterans.

Five Indianans have served as vice president of the United States

SCHUYLER COLFAX (1869–1873)
Seventeenth vice president in the Republican administration of Ulysses S. Grant. Colfax moved to Indiana in his early youth.

THOMAS A. HENDRICKS (1885)
Twenty-first vice president in the Democratic administration of Grover Cleveland. Hendricks was born in Ohio, but began his career in Indiana.

CHARLES W. FAIRBANKS (1905–1909)
Twenty-sixth vice president in the Republican administration of Theodore Roosevelt. Like Hendricks before him, Fairbanks was born in Ohio but began his legal and political career in Indiana.

THOMAS MARSHALL (1913–1921)
Twenty-eighth vice president in the Democratic administration of Woodrow Wilson.

DAN QUAYLE (1989–1993) Forty-fourth vice president in the Republican administration of George Bush.

Each of Indiana's ninety-two counties (except one) is run by a three-member board of elected commissioners. Townships are governed by officials called Township Trustees. Municipalities and school districts are led by elected officials.

DID YOU KNOW?

Eugene V. Debs from Terre Haute was the Socialist Party candidate for U.S. president five times — in 1900, 1904, 1908, 1912, and 1920.

Fine Arts and Fast Cars

> When I was born in 1922, barely a hundred years after Indiana became the 19th state in the Union, the Middle West already boasted a constellation of cities with symphony orchestras and museums and libraries, and institutions of higher learning, and schools of music and art, reminiscent of the Austro-Hungarian Empire before the First World War. One could almost say that Chicago was our Vienna, Indianapolis our Prague, Cincinnati our Budapest and Cleveland our Bucharest.
>
> — *Kurt Vonnegut*, "To Be a Native Middle Westerner"

The Arts Scene

For an industrial state that relies on manufacturing and agriculture for its income, Indiana really packs an arts and entertainment punch. World-renowned authors, actors, artists, and sports legends call Indiana home.

When it comes to the arts, chances are Indiana has touched your life. Frank Baum wrote his famous *Wizard of Oz* in Indiana, Janet Jackson and her famous brothers got their start here, and "Garfield the Cat" was written and drawn by Indiana's Jim Davis. Writers include James Whitcomb Riley, Booth Tarkington, Theodore Dreiser, and Lew Wallace.

Name That Tune

Indiana is steeped in musical culture. With more than thirty symphony orchestras and

▼ Dorothy and Glinda the Good Witch, in MGM's 1939 film of Frank Baum's *The Wizard of Oz.*

countless singing groups, Indiana hums along. Memorable songs such as Albert von Tilzer's "Take Me Out to the Ball Game," Cole Porter's "Night and Day," John Cougar Mellencamp's "Fire and Ice," Michael Jackson's "Thriller," and Janet Jackson's "Together Again," were all made famous by musicians who call Indiana home.

Native Indianans such as David Letterman or Red Skelton have probably made you laugh, and old-time movie stars such as James Dean, Steve McQueen, and Carole Lombard lit up the screen in their day.

Where Basketball Is King

Basketball rules in Indiana. It is popular on every level — high school, college, and professional. Indiana claims to have more basketball hoops per capita than any other state. There is even one in the driveway of the governor's executive mansion! Almost every Indianan seems to participate in Hoosier Hysteria, the state's annual high-school basketball tournament. Some of the best players in the country have first been noticed in this event.

Indiana University's basketball team — also nicknamed

▲ Indiana Pacers guard Reggie Miller goes for a shot.

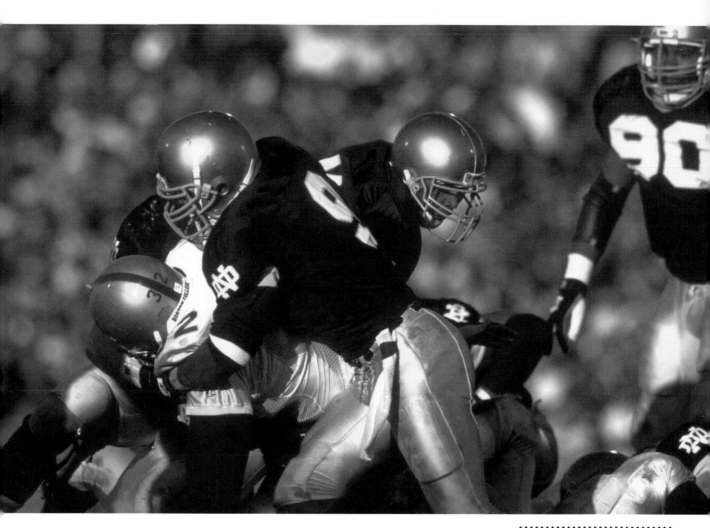

the Hoosiers — commands great enthusiasm not only in the state but also nationwide. Famous alumni include some of the sport's best, such as Isiah Thomas and Alan Henderson.

The Indiana Pacers, the state's pro-basketball franchise, was formerly coached by native son Larry Bird. Bird earned his own basketball immortality as one of the sport's greatest players of all time. He led his team, the Boston Celtics, to win the National Basketball Association (NBA) Championship in 1981, 1984, and 1986. Bird's efforts also earned him the Most Valuable Player (MVP) award in 1984, 1985, and 1986. In 1998 his skill was deservedly recognized with his induction into the Basketball Hall of Fame. With Bird as their coach, the Pacers became one of the top teams in the NBA. In 2000 the team reached the finals of the NBA championships.

▲ It's Notre Dame versus Boston College.

DID YOU KNOW?

The first baseball game at night was played in 1883 at League Park in Fort Wayne, Indiana. The field was illuminated by seventeen lights of 4,000 candlepower each.

Notre Dame: Where Legends Are Born

Every football fan knows where the "Fighting Irish" live — the University of Notre Dame in South Bend, Indiana. One of the best known and most well-loved teams, Notre Dame has contributed more than four hundred players to professional football — more than any other college or university team.

Notre Dame's football team has drawn national attention ever since the 1920s, the decade often referred to as the golden age of sports. The famous coach, Knute Rockne, taught his players speed, ball-handling skill, and the importance of dedication and teamwork. It worked. America had never seen this kind of playing before, and the Fighting Irish were unstoppable.

Win One for the Gipper

George Gipp was a star athlete on Knute Rockne's team. His speed, agility, and grace set him apart from every other player. He could pass, he could punt, and he could run. Everybody cheered when he was on the field. He could do no wrong.

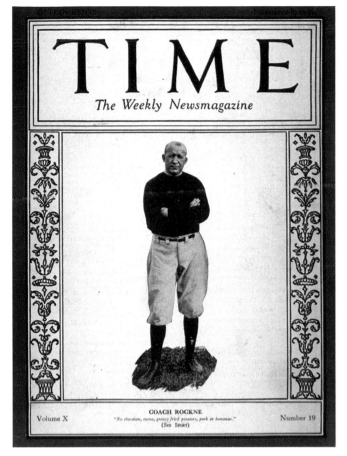

TIME
The Weekly Newsmagazine

Volume X

COACH ROCKNE
"No chocolate, cocoa, greasy fried potatoes, pork or bananas."
(See Sport)

Number 19

▲ Knute Rockne graces the cover of *Time* magazine.

▼ The Indy 500.

Sport	Team	Home
Basketball	Indiana Pacers	Conseco Fieldhouse, Indianapolis
Women's Basketball	Indiana Fever	Conseco Fieldhouse, Indianapolis
Football	Indianapolis Colts	RCA Dome, Indianapolis
Hockey	Indiana Firebirds	Conseco Fieldhouse, Indianapolis

Hollywood even made a movie about Gipp starring Ronald Reagan. Unfortunately, his stardom was bright and short-lived; he died at age twenty-five of pneumonia. Rockne never forgot his star player, and neither did his teammates. When the team was ready to go onto the field to play, Rockne was known to say, "Win one for the Gipper."

The Indy 500

Mention car racing anywhere and the first thing that comes to mind is the Indianapolis 500 — the most famous car-racing event in the world. Every Memorial Day since 1911, thousands of people come from all over the world to the Indianapolis Motor Speedway to watch racers from as far away as Israel and Germany burn rubber and zip around the track for 500 miles (804 km) as they race and roar at dizzying speeds.

Tennis Anyone?

The U.S. Clay Court Championships, held in Indianapolis, attract top international tennis players every year. In 1987 Indianapolis became the second U.S. city to host the Pan-American Games. These games are a direct result of

New Harmony

In 1825, Robert Owen, a wealthy British reformer, came to Indiana to found a Utopian community, which he named New Harmony. It was based on lofty principles of rational thinking and cooperation but initially proved an expensive failure. Later, however, it developed into a notable scientific and cultural center. A laboratory, built by one of Robert Owen's sons, David Dale Owen, was headquarters for what later became the U.S. Geological Survey.

President Benjamin Harrison's policies to strengthen ties between the United States and Central America.

Recreation

Brimming with mighty industry, quiet farmland, and bustling cities, Indiana is also graced with beautiful rivers and lakes, rolling landscapes, underground caves, and lush forests. The state has twenty-four state parks where bikers, hikers, boaters, explorers, and cross-country-skiers can take advantage of nature's beauty.

The state also has many museums that exhibit a variety of interesting collections, from the Levi Coffin House, a stop on the Underground Railroad, and the Lincoln Boyhood National Memorial, which commemorates the childhood farm home of Abraham Lincoln, to car racing history at the Speedway Museum in Indianapolis and antique cars at the Auburn-Cord-Duesenberg Museum. There is always something to do and see in Indiana.

Native Middle Westerners

> To grow up in such a city, as I did, was to find cultural institutions as ordinary as police stations or fire houses. So it was reasonable for a young person to daydream of becoming some sort of artist or intellectual, if not a policeman or fireman. So I did. So did many like me . . .
>
> — *Kurt Vonnegut, "To Be a Native Middle Westerner"*

Following are only a few of the thousands of people who lived, died, or spent most of their lives in Indiana and had an extraordinary effect on the state and the nation.

WILBUR WRIGHT
INVENTOR AND AVIATOR

BORN: *April 16, 1867, Millville*
DIED: *May 30, 1912, Dayton, OH*

Wilbur Wright was born in Indiana, and with his younger brother and inventing partner, Orville (born in nearby Dayton, Ohio), became part of one of the most famous inventing teams of all time. They built and flew the world's first airplane. Wilbur designed the flying machine with wings to provide lift, a power source for propulsion, and a system of control. In August of 1900 Wilbur built his first glider. In 1903 he and his brother built an engine-driven flying machine. While Wilbur got the first chance to fly the machine, it stalled and sustained minor damage. His brother Orville was given the second chance — and on December 17, 1903, at Kitty Hawk, North Carolina, Orville Wright made the first machine-powered flight in the world.

COLE (ALBERT) PORTER
COMPOSER AND MUSICIAN

BORN: *June 9, 1891, Peru*
DIED: *October 15, 1964, Santa Monica, CA*

Cole Porter brought worldly sophistication to American popular music. A child prodigy, Porter had his first musical composition published when he was just eleven. By the time he was a student at Yale University, he had composed about three hundred songs. In 1928 Porter began composing musical comedies for the stage, including *Anything Goes* (1934); *Red, Hot and Blue* (1934); and *Kiss Me, Kate* (1948). Porter wrote a staggering

number of classic songs, including "I've Got You Under My Skin."

John (Herbert) Dillinger
BANK ROBBER

BORN: *June 28, 1902 or June 22, 1903, Indianapolis*
DIED: *July 22, 1934, Chicago, IL*

Most famous of all U.S. bank robbers, his career of daring robberies and even more daring escapes made him a legend. Dillinger first rose to fame after he robbed five Indiana and Ohio banks in four months. He was arrested but escaped to rob more banks. This became his pattern. In his most famous escape, Dillinger carved a fake pistol out of wood, blackened it with shoe polish, and bluffed his way past a dozen guards. Finally, the FBI and the Indiana Police joined forces and convinced a lady friend of Dillinger's to lure him to the Biograph Theatre in Chicago, where he was shot to death by police.

Carole Lombard
ACTRESS

BORN: *October 6, 1908, Fort Wayne*
DIED: *January 16, 1942, near Las Vegas, NV*

Carole Lombard was a movie star from the golden age of the silver screen. Lombard managed to be both a dramatic actress and the queen of early screwball comedies. Some of her famous movies included *My Man Godfrey* (1936) and *To Be Or Not To Be* (1942). She was married to two other famous movie stars — William Powell and Clark Gable. Unfortunately, Lombard's career and life were cut short when her plane crashed as she toured in support of the fundraising effort for World War II.

Jimmy Hoffa
UNION LEADER

BORN: *February 14, 1913, Brazil*
DIED: *disappeared July 30, 1975, Bloomfield Hills, near Detroit, MI*

James Riddle Hoffa was a U.S. labor leader who served as president of the International Brotherhood of Teamsters Union from 1957 to 1971. The son of an Indiana coal driller, Hoffa began organizing unions in the 1930s, ultimately helping to make the Teamsters the largest labor union in the United States. Hoffa, however, was known to have associated with various criminal and underworld figures, and in 1967 he was arrested and sentenced to a thirteen-year prison term for jury tampering, fraud, and conspiracy. After his jail sentence was cut short in 1971, Jimmy Hoffa mysteriously disappeared from a restaurant near Detroit in 1975. His disappearance has never been explained, and he was legally "presumed dead" in 1982.

James Dean
ACTOR

BORN: *February 8, 1931, Marion*
DIED: *September 30, 1955, Paso Robles, CA*

James Dean was a popular movie star who made a huge impact on American popular culture in the 1950s with the films *East of Eden, Giant,* and *Rebel Without a Cause.* Dean's energy and open displays of emotional intensity seemed to tap perfectly into the mindset of the emergent youth culture at the time. James Dean died in an auto crash at the age of twenty-four.

KURT VONNEGUT
WRITER

BORN: *November 11, 1922, Indianapolis*

Kurt Vonnegut is a renowned novelist and proud Midwesterner. As a young man, Vonnegut served in the Second World War and was captured during the Battle of the Bulge in 1944. This experience became the basis for his most famous novel, *Slaughterhouse Five* (1969), which was both a bestseller and a critically acclaimed movie. Other famous Vonnegut novels include *Cat's Cradle* (1963), *God Bless You, Mr. Rosewater* (1965), and *Breakfast of Champions* (1973). Vonnegut was named State Author for New York in November of 2000.

DAVID LETTERMAN
ENTERTAINER

BORN: *April 12, 1947, Indianapolis*

During his childhood in Indianapolis, David Letterman was a big fan of Johnny Carson who hosted *The Tonight Show Starring Johnny Carson,* which was the top-rated night-time show for thirty years. Letterman graduated from Ball State University, where he majored in telecommunications and immediately began working in radio and television in the Indianapolis area. He was a news anchor, a weatherman, and host of a children's show. In 1975 he moved to Los Angeles and began working as a stand-up comedian. Three years later he made his first appearance on the

Johnny Carson show. He went on to guest-host the show fifty times before becoming host of his own show on NBC in 1982, *Late Night with David Letterman.* It became very popular and won a George Foster Peabody Award in 1992 and two Emmy Awards. The show included nightly top-ten lists with silly themes, viewer mail, and a segment called "Stupid Pet Tricks." In 1993, Letterman moved to CBS and began hosting *The Late Show with David Letterman,* which remains among the top-rated shows on television and has won eight Emmy Awards.

LARRY BIRD
ATHLETE

BORN: *December 7, 1956, West Baden*

Larry Bird is considered one of the greatest basketball players of all time. He and Magic Johnson brought new life to the NBA during the 1980s with a competitive rivalry between their respective teams, the Boston Celtics and the Los Angeles Lakers. Bird has won every major award professional basketball offers. He was voted Most Valuable Player in 1984, 1985, and 1986, was named to the All-NBA First Team for nine consecutive seasons, and was a twelve-time NBA All-Star. Bird was also a member of the "Dream Team" that won a gold medal at the Barcelona Olympics in 1992. Bird set new standards for skill, becoming the first player in NBA history to shoot over 50 percent from the field and over 90 percent from the foul line. He retired from the game in 1992 and has since been inducted into the Basketball Hall of Fame. He coached the Pacers back in his home state of Indiana.

MICHAEL JACKSON

SINGER AND POP STAR

BORN: *August 29, 1958, Gary*

Michael Jackson was the seventh of nine children. His father, a steel-mill worker, decided to form a singing group called the Jackson Five. Only five years old when the group started, Michael was at first only a novelty. Soon he became the star. The Jackson Five had six top-five singles between 1969 and 1971, including "I Want You Back" and "ABC." In 1971, at the age of fourteen, Michael made his first solo record, "I'll Be There," which hit number four on the charts. In 1982 Jackson rocketed to the top of the charts with his mega-album *Thriller* (1982), the best-selling album of all time. It sold forty million copies, received eight Grammy Awards, and spawned six top-ten singles. The *Thriller* album also helped usher in the new age of music video. Jackson's subsequent albums, *Bad* (1987) and *Dangerous* (1991), also both topped the charts, though Jackson began to get some negative media attention for his many plastic surgery procedures and eccentric personal habits. Still, the release of the 1995 album, *HIStory*, was greeted with worldwide excitement, and Jackson remains one of the most famous recording artists of the twentieth century.

JANET JACKSON

SINGER AND POP STAR

BORN: *May 16, 1966, Gary*

While known today as a singer (and as the younger sister of Michael Jackson and her other brothers in the Jackson Five), Janet Jackson started her career as an actress, playing Willona's adopted daughter, Penny, on the sitcom *Good Times*. Other roles followed, but in the 1980s, she managed to get out of the shadow of her famous brothers and become a singer in her own right. Her record "Control" was her breakthrough, and albums like *Rhythm Nation 1814* and *The Velvet Rope* have kept her at the top of the charts.

▼ Hoosier hits the big-time. David Letterman's *Late Show* studio in New York City.

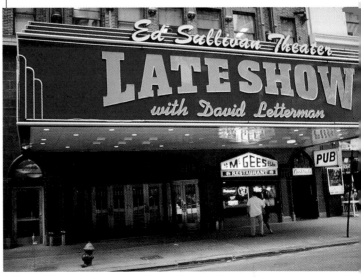

Indiana
History At-A-Glance

1541
Spanish explorer Hernando de Soto enters the town of the lord of Casqui (Vincennes) and visits Aquixo (Angel Mounds).

1686
Kekionga, later known as "Miami Town," and currently known as Fort Wayne, becomes a trading post.

1763
British take control of the area that includes Indiana.

1673
La Salle enters the St. Joseph River; previously thought to be the first European visit to Indiana.

1763–64
Chief Pontiac and Native American warriors capture most of the Trans-Allegheny forts, including Fort Miami.

1777
Native Americans on the Trans-Appalachian Frontier encouraged by the British to attack frontier Americans.

1783
U.S. gains control of Indiana territory.

1787
The Continental Congress enacts the Northwest Ordinance.

1800
Indiana Territory established from the Northwest Territory; William Henry Harrison is the first governor and Vincennes the capital.

1804
Vincennes serves as the capital of the Louisiana Purchase for nine months.

1600   **1700**   **1800**

1492
Christopher Columbus comes to New World.

1607
Capt. John Smith and three ships land on Virginia coast and start first English settlement in New World — Jamestown.

1754–63
French and Indian War.

1773
Boston Tea Party.

1776
Declaration of Independence adopted July 4.

1777
Articles of Confederation adopted by Continental Congress.

1787
U.S. Constitution written.

1812–14
War of 1812.

United States
History At-A-Glance

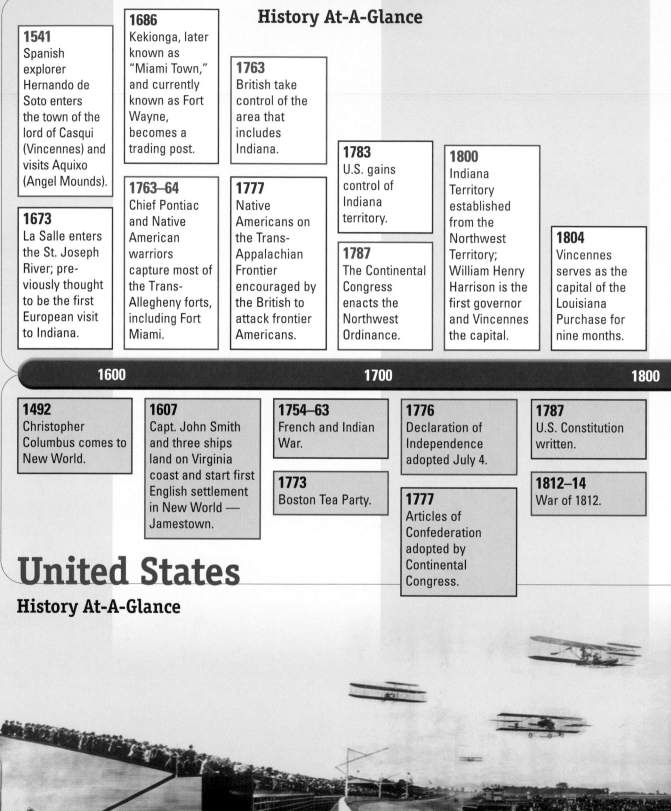

1804
Elihu Stout prints the laws of the Territory, and the *Indiana Gazette,* Indiana's first newspaper, is established.

1805
Michigan Territory separates from Indiana Territory.

1809
Illinois Territory separates from Indiana Territory.

1816
Indiana becomes a state, with the capital at Corydon; Jonathan Jennings (1784–1834) becomes the first governor of the state of Indiana.

1825
Indianapolis becomes the capital of Indiana.

1846
Miami tribe leaves Indiana for Kansas Territory.

1851
Indiana adopts a state constitution that includes a measure protecting the property rights of married women; this same constitution governs Indiana today.

1881
The American Federation of Labor (AFL) is organized in Terre Haute.

1889
Benjamin Harrison becomes the twenty-third U.S. president.

1911
The first long-distance auto race in the U.S. is held at the Indianapolis Motor Speedway.

1972
Indiana University's greatest swimmer, Mark Spitz, wins seven gold medals in the Olympic games; no other athlete has won so many gold medals in a single year.

1987
Indianapolis becomes the second U.S. city to host the Pan-American Games.

1800   **1900**   **2000**

1848
Gold discovered in California draws 80,000 prospectors in the 1849 Gold Rush.

1861–65
Civil War.

1869
Transcontinental Railroad completed.

1917–18
U.S. involvement in World War I.

1929
Stock market crash ushers in Great Depression.

1941–45
U.S. involvement in World War II.

1950–53
U.S. fights in the Korean War.

1964–73
U.S. involvement in Vietnam War.

2000
George W. Bush wins the closest presidential election in history.

2001
A terrorist attack in which four hijacked airliners crash into New York City's World Trade Center, the Pentagon, and farmland in western Pennsylvania leaves thousands dead or injured.

▼ **An aviation meet held at the Indianapolis Motor Speedway in 1910.**

Festivals and Fun For All

Check web site for exact date and directions.

500 Festival, Indianapolis

Rev up your engines for motor-racing excitement — a month of events celebrating the Indy 500, the greatest racing spectacle in the world.
www.500festival.com/

Circus City Festival, Peru

Each July approximately two hundred and fifty young people ages seven to twenty-one present ten performances.
www.perucircus.com/

The Feast of the Hunters' Moon, Lafayette

Re-create the autumn fur-trading gathering between the French and Native Americans, which took place at Fort Ouiatanon in the mid-1700s.
www.tcha.mus.in.us/feast.htm

Glass Festival, Elwood

Crafts and flea market booths, food, entertainment, a vintage car show, glass factory tours, and more!
www.elwood.org/festivals.htm

Indiana State Fair, Indianapolis

For a dozen days each summer, over seven hundred and fifty thousand people visit the Indiana State Fair for extraordinary fun.
www.IN.gov/statefair/

Firefly Festival, South Bend

Enjoy jazz, blues, musical theater, Irish dance, R&B, pop, country, comedy, and more!
www.fireflyfestival.com/

Johnny Appleseed Festival, Fort Wayne

Since the first gathering on the riverbank in 1976, the Johnny Appleseed Festival has embraced the sights, sounds, smells, and flavors of the early 1800s.
johnnyappleseedfest.com/

Mentone Egg Festival, Mentone

Celebrating Mentone as the egg capital of the world.
www.indianafestivals.org/spring.html

Remembering James Dean Festival, Fairmount

Celebrating the life and times of James Dean with a look-alike contest, cars, food, and films.
www.jamesdeanartifacts.com

Mushroom Festival, Mansfield

A mushroom hunt, contest, car show, food, and flea market make up this festival in historic Mansfield.

mansfieldvillage.com/mansfield

Tree City Fall Festival, Greensburg

Celebrating the mysterious tree that grows out of the Decatur County Courthouse roof (with no visible means of nutrition)!

www.treecityfallfestival.com/

Bill Monroe Memorial Bluegrass Festival, Bean Blossom

Bluegrass music in celebration of Bill Monroe, the country star of the 1930s and '40s.

www.beanblossom.com/OurFestivals/Memorial.html

Valparaiso Popcorn Festival, Valparaiso

Celebrating popcorn and Indiana's own Orville Redenbacher.

www.popcornfest.org/

Wizard of Oz Festival, Chesterton

Join some of the original Munchkins and celebrate the Wizard of Oz in the town where Frank Baum is thought to have written his famous story.

www.cebunet.com/oz/

Many Coats of Color, Alexandria

Two brothers created the largest ball of paint in the world by coating a baseball with over fourteen thousand layers of paint. The ball is 80 inches (203 cm) and growing!

Philip Robinson Fruit Jar Museum, Muncie

Home to world's largest collection of jars.

The Windmills Museum, Kendalville

The nation's one and only.

www.midamericawindmillmuseum.com

The Land of Limestone Museum, Bedford

Learn how Lawrence County's famous limestone was used in landmark buildings across the country.

www.ai.org/tourism/media/ideas/museums.html

Wizard of Oz Museum, Chesterton

Stroll through the Yellow Brick Road Gift Shop and browse in the Museum.

www.yellowbrickroadonline.com

Dan Quayle Center and Museum, Huntington

Over six thousand Quayle artifacts, such as a lock of Quayle's baby hair and his third-grade report card.

www.quaylemuseum.org

RV/MH Hall of Fame, Elkhart

Learn about the history and evolution of the recreational vehicle.

www.rv-mh-hall-of-fame.org

Books

Conway, W. Fred. *Young Abe Lincoln: His Teenage Years in Indiana.* New Albany, IN: Fire Buff House, 1992. The sixteenth president's early life in Indiana.

Crenshaw, Gwendolyn J. *Bury Me in a Free Land: the Abolitionist Movement in Indiana,* 1816-1865. Indianapolis: Indiana Historical Bureau, 1986. Learn about Indianans who worked to end slavery in the nineteenth century.

Fradin, Dennis Brindell and Judith B. Fradin. *Indiana.* Danbury, CT: Children's Press, 1995. Facts and figures about Indiana's past and present.

Italia, Bob. *Inside the NBA: The Indiana Pacers.* Edina, MN: Abdo & Daughters, 1997. The story of a world champion team.

Kitchel, Thomas W. *Growing up in Indiana: Memories of a Hoosier Farmboy.* Edina, MN; Spring Lake, MI: River Road Books, 1992. Learn what life was like on an Indiana farm in the 1920s.

McKenna, A.T. *Fast Tracks: Indy Racing.* Edina, MN: Abdo & Daughters, 1998. What it takes to be an Indiana-500 driver.

Shorto, Russell. *Tecumseh and the Dream of an American Indian Nation.* Englewood Cliffs, NJ: Silver Burdett, 1989. A biography of a Native American hero and his battle with William Henry Harrison.

Web Sites

▶ Official state web site
www.state.in.us

▶ Official capital site
www.indygov.org

▶ Official Indy-500 Web site
www.indy500.com

▶ The Indiana Historical Society
www.indianahistory.org

Films

Harnett, Kendall and Doug Haight. *FreeWheels: Fifty Years of the Little 500.* Evanston, IL: Kendall Harnett and Doug Haight, 2001. Learn the history of Indiana's famous bicycle race.

WCTY Hoosier History Series. *Indiana's African American Community.* Indianapolis, IN: Indiana State Library, 1990. Indianapolis's rich African-American history.

INDEX

Note: Page numbers in *italics* refer to illustrations or photographs.

A

African-Americans, 13, 17. *See also* slavery; Underground Railroad
age distribution, *17*
agriculture, 14–15, 20–21, 26–27
airports, 27
American Railway Union, 7, 26
The American Tragedy (Vonnegut), 4
Amish, 17, *17*
Anderson, Elijah, 13
Angel Mounds, 8–9
area (square miles), 6
arts, 32–33, 36, 38, 39
attractions
   Amish and Mennonite country, *17*
   capitol building, *29*
   festivals, 44–45
   Indiana Dunes National Lakeshore, 23, *23*
   Indianapolis Motor Speedway, *4–5,* 15, *35, 36, 42,* 44, *44,*
   Levi Coffin House, *14,* 37
   Lincoln Boyhood National Memorial, 7, 37
   museums, 37, *37,* 45
   parks and memorials, 7, 23
   sports, 33, *33,* 34, *34,* 35, *35,* 36, 40
   Wyandotte Caves, 7, 23
Auburn-Cord-Deusenberg Museum, 37
automobile industry, 15. *See also* Indianapolis Motor Speedway
aviation, 38

B

Ball Jar Company, 15, 26
Ball State University, 26
basketball, 33, *33,* 34, 40
Basketball Hall Of Fame, 34, 40
Battle Ground, Indiana, 11
Battle of Tippecanoe, 11
Bayh, Evan, 28
Bill Monroe Memorial Bluegrass Festival, 43
Bird, Larry, 34, 40
bird (state bird), 6
books about Indiana, 46
Burnside, Ambrose, 7

C

"Can't Get Indiana Off My Mind" (de Leon), 8
capital, *5,* 6, 28–29
capitol building, *29*
cardinal (state bird), 6
caves, 23
Central Plains, 21
Chief Pontiac, 12
Circus City Festival, 44
cities, *5,* 6, 19
Civil War, 13–14
climate, 21
Coffin, Katie, *13,* 13–14
Coffin, Levi, 13–14
Colfax, Schuyler, *31*
commerce. *See* economy; industry
compact discs, 24, *26*
Constitution of Indiana, 28–29
Continental Congress, 12
counties, 30-31
courts, 30
culture, 32–37. *See also* attractions

D

Dan Quayle Center and Museum, 45
Dana, Edmund, 20
Davis, Jim, 32
de Leon, Robert, 8
de Soto, Hernando, 9
Dean, James, 4, 19, 39
Debs, Eugene V., 24, 26, 31
Declaration of Independence, 31
Dependent Pension Act, 31
Dillinger, John (Herbert), 39
Dreiser, Theodore, 4, 19

E

economy. *See also* industry
   agriculture, 14–15, 20–21, 26–27
   automobile industry, 15
   employers, *24*
   fur trade, 10
   Gas Belt, 26
   gross state product, *25*
   highways, 4, *5,* 27
   Maumee-Wabash trade route, 10–11
   natural resources, 26
   nuclear power, 26
   politics and, 28
   railroads, 27
   steel production, 7, 15, *26*
   unions, 7, 26, 39
education levels, *18*
electoral votes, *28*
electric street lights, 7
elevation, 20, *21, 22*
Elkhart, Indiana, 7, 24
employers, *24*
ethnic groups, 16-17, *16, 17*
Evansville, 6
executive branch of government, 29
explorers, 9–10

F

Fairbanks, Charles W., *31*
farming, 14–15, 20–21, 26–27
Feast of the Hunters' Moon, 44
festivals, 44–45
"Fighting Irish," 35
films about Indiana, 46
Firefly Festival, 44
500 Festival, 44
flower (state flower), 6
football, 35-36
Fort Industry, 12
Fort Ouiatanon, 11
Fort Philippe, 11
Fort Saint Louis, 11
Fort Vincennes, 11
Fort Wayne, 6, *10,* 12, 13, 24
Fort Wayne International Airport, 27
Fountain City, 13
French and Indian Wars, 11, 16
Frontenac, Louis de Baude de, 10
fur trade, 10

G

Gary, 6
Gas Belt, 26
General Assembly, 29
geography, 20–23
Gipp, George, 35
Glass Festival, 44
glass-making, 26, 44
goldfish, 7
government, 28–31
Grand Central Station, 13–14
Great Lakes plains, 21
gross state product, *25*
Grouseland, Indiana, 12

H

Harrison, Benjamin, 30, *31*
Harrison, William Henry, 12-13, 23, 31
Hendricks, Thomas A., *31*
highest point, *21, 22*
highways, 4, *5,* 27
hills, 22–23
hockey, 35

Hoffa, Jimmy, 26, 39
Holiday World Theme Park, 7
Hoosier Hysteria, 33
"Hoosiers," 4, 5, 15
Huron Indians, 11

I

Illinois Indians, 11
immigrants, 17
Indiana Dunes National Lakeshore, 23, *23,* 27
Indiana Pacers, *33,* 34
Indiana State Fair, 44
Indiana State seal, 28
Indianapolis, 13, 18-19, 28, 36
Indianapolis International Airport, 27
Indianapolis Motor Speedway, *4–5,* 15, *35,* 36, *42,* 44, *44*
industry, *see also* economy
   automobile industry, 15
   employers, *24*
   fur trade, 10
   glass-making, 26
   gross state product, *25*
   highways, 4, *5,* 27
   limestone quarries, 6, 14, 26
   musical instrument manufacturing, 7, 24
   natural resources, 26
   nuclear power, 26
   politics and, 28
   railroads, 27
   steel production, 7, 15, *26*
   transportation, 27
   unions, 7, 26, 39
insect (state insect), 6
International Brotherhood of Teamsters, 39
Interstate Highway system, 4, *5,* 27
Iroquois Indians, 11

J

Jackson Five, 19, 41
Jackson, Janet, 33, 41, *41*
Jackson, Michael, 33, 41, *41*
Jennings, Jonathan, 13
Johnny Appleseed Festival, 44
judicial branch of government, 30

L

La Salle, Robert Cavelier sieur de, 9–10
Lake Erie, 23
lakes, 23

The Land of Limestone Museum, 43
landscape, *22*
Late Show studio, 41
Laulewasikau, 11, *11*
legislative branch of government, 29
Letterman, David, 4, 16, 40, *41*
Levi Coffin House, *14,* 37
limestone, 6, 14–15, 26
Lincoln, Abraham, 12, 14, 16
Lincoln Boyhood National Memorial, 7, 37
local government, 30
Lombard, Carole, 39
Lost River, 7
lowlands, 22–23

M

manufacturing, 24–26. *See also* industry
maps of Indiana, *5, 22, 25*
Marengo Caves, 23
Marshall, Thomas, *31*
Maumee River, *22,* 23
Maumee-Wabash trade route, 10–11
McQueen, Steve, 4
Mennonites, 17
Mentone Egg Festival, 44
Miami Indians, 11
"Miami Town," 10–11
Middle Mississippian culture, 8
Midwestern Corn Belt, 21
Miller, Reggie, *33*
Mississippi River, 11, 27
motto (state motto), 6
museums, 37, *37,* 45
Mushroom Festival, 45
music, 32–33, 36, 38, 41, 45
musical instrument manufacturing, 7, 24

N

naming of Indiana, 16
Native Americans, 8, 11, 16
natural resources, 26
New Harmony, *9,* 36
New Harmony on the Wabash (Maximilian), *9*
Northern Lake and Moraine Region, 21
Northwest Ordinance, 12
Northwest Territory, 12–13
nuclear power, 26

O

O'Bannon, Frank, 28
Ohio River, 8, 23, 27
Outawa Indians, 11
Owen, David Dale, 36
Owen, Robert, 36

P

Pan-American Conference, 31
Pan-American Games, 35
peony (state flower), 6, *6*
Philip Robinson Fruit Jar Museum, 43
poem (state poem), 6
politics and political figures
  Bannon, Frank, 28
  Bayh, Evan, 28
  branches of government, 29–30
  Burnside, Ambrose, 7
  Colfax, Schuyler, *31*
  counties, 30, 31
  courts, 30
  Debs, Eugene, 24, 26, 31
  Fairbanks, Charles W., *31*
  Harrison, Benjamin, 30, *31,*
  Harrison, William Henry, 12-13, 23, 31
  Hendricks, Thomas A., *31*
  Hoffa, Jimmy, 26, 39
  Lincoln, Abraham, 12, 14, 16
  Marshall, Thomas, *31*
  Quayle, Dan, *31,* 45
  Township Trustee, 30-*31*
  vice presidents, 30-*31*
popcorn, *27*
population, 6
Port of Indiana, 27
Porter, Cole (Albert), 4, 38

Q

Quakers, 13
Quayle, Dan, *31,* 45

R

racial backgrounds, *17*
railroads, 27
rainfall, *21*
Reagan, Ronald, 36
recreation, 37
recreational vehicles, *45*
religious affiliations, *19*
Remembering James Dean Festival, 44
Riley, James Whitcomb, 32
rivers
  Lost River, 7
  Maumee River, *22,* 23
  Mississippi River, 11, 27
  Ohio River, 8, 23, 27
  St. Joseph River, 23
  St. Marys River, 23
  Tippecanoe River, *22,* 23
  Wabash River, *22*
  White River, *22,* 23
Rockne, Knute, 35
RV/MH Hall of Fame, 45

S

sand dunes, 23
Say's firefly, 6
Seignelay, Marquis de, 11
settlers, 13, 16–17
Slaughterhouse Five (Vonnegut), 4, 40
slavery, 4, 13–14
snowfall, *20*
Socialist Party, *30*
song (state song), 6
South Bend, 6
South Bend Regional Airport, 27
sports, 33, *33,* 34, *34,* 35, *35,* 36, 40
St. Joseph River, 23
St. Lawrence Seaway, 27
St. Mary River, 23
statehood, 6, 13–14
state symbols, 6
steel production, 7, 15, *26*
stone (state stone), 6
Studebaker automobile, *15*
symbols of Indiana, 6

T

Tarkington, Booth, 32
Teamsters Union, 26
temperature, *21*
tennis, 37
Tenskwatawa, 11, *11*
theme parks, 7
Thriller (Jackson), 33, 41
Till Plains, 21
timeline of Indiana history, 42–43
Tippecanoe River, *22,* 23
"To Be a Native Middle Westerner" (Vonnegut), 18, 32, 40
tourism. *See* attractions
towns, *5,* 19. *See also* cities
Township Trustee, 30-31
transportation, 4, 27
Treaty of Fort Greenville, *12*
Treaty of Paris, 12
Tree City Fall Festival, 45
tree (state tree), 6
tulip poplar tree, 6

U

Underground Railroad, 4, 13–14, 37
unions, 7, 26, 39
University of Notre Dame, 35–36
U.S. Clay Court Championships, 36

V

The Valparaiso Popcorn Festival, 45

vice presidents, 30-*31*
Vonnegut, Kurt, 4, 18, 32, 40
voting, 28

W

Wabash, Indiana, 7
Wabash River, *22*
Wallace, Lew, 32
Warden, David Baillie, 21
Web sites about Indiana, 46
White River, *22,* 23
The Windmills Museum, 45
Wizard of Oz, 32, *32*
The Wizard of Oz Festival, 45
The Wizard of Oz Museum, 45
Wright, Orville, 4, 38
Wright, Wilbur, 4, 38
Wyandotte Caves, 7, 23